MORE THAN ORDINARY

choices:

making good decisions

KIT AND DREW COONS

More Than Ordinary Choices: Making Good Decisions

© 2018 Kit and Drew Coons

ISBN: 978-0-9995689-8-9

Unless otherwise noted, all Scripture quotations are taken from the New American Standard Bible (NASB). Copyright © 1960, 1962, 1963, 1968, 1971, 1972, 1973, 1975, 1977, 1995 by The Lockman Foundation

Edited by Jayna Richardson
Design: Julie Sullivan (MerakiLifeDesigns.com)

First Edition
Printed in the United States

22 21 20 19 18   1 2 3 4 5

contents

Poor Choices Affect Lives 1

Start with the Premise that You Are Not Wise 5
Solomon's Overconfidence
A Misleading Biblical Interpretation
Acquiring Wisdom and Understanding

Worldly Wisdom 17
"Always Follow Your Heart"
"No Time Like the Present"
"Never Admit a Mistake"

The Importance of Counselors. 27
The Right Counselors
The Wrong Counselors

**God's Word Correctly Interpreted
Leads to the Best Choices** 35
Choices Before a Crisis
Danger in Misunderstanding the Bible
Cultural Bias in Interpretation
Personal Bias in Interpretation
Finding the Most Accurate Interpretation

All Truth is God's Truth. 45
Objectively Evaluate Alternatives
Avoid Acting Rashly
Take Some Chances

Beware of Second Guessing Yourself. 53

POOR CHOICES
affect lives

"I'm going to prison," the father of three told us. The businessman had committed a white-collar crime, something about taxes that only an accountant might understand.

His wife stood beside him. "I . . . am . . . so . . . angry . . . at . . . him," she said through clenched teeth. Soon and unexpectedly she would have three children to care for alone and without a source of income. Even after his release from prison in about three years, the family's upper-middle-class livelihood had been destroyed.

The occasion was a two-day Christian marriage conference we led in North Carolina. The husband had made a poor choice, and the entire family would suffer for it. Although God can work miracles, survival of their marriage seemed unlikely as well, compounding the future grief. Poor choices can prevent people from leading the more than ordinary lives they desire.

1

Every moment separates our lives into before and after. Some moments divide our lives into never before and always after. Many of those life-changing moments are based on the choices we make. God allows us to make choices through free will. Most awake moments include minor decisions. Some decisions are more consequential and will affect the remainder of our lives. Making good choices at those moments is for our good and ultimately reflects on God as we represent Him in this world.

The Bible is full of instances where men and women made poor choices that diminished their lives and frequently the lives of others. David sinned with Bathsheba, which divided his family (2 Samuel 11); he numbered the people, resulting in the deaths of many (2 Samuel 24:10); and he failed to discipline his sons (1 Kings 1:6), leading to the deaths of several. Surprisingly, these bad decisions came from a man who truly loved God. The Children of Israel made a poor choice not to trust God and enter the Promised Land the first time and thereby died in the desert (Joshua 5:6).

The New Testament also has many examples of poor choices. Consider the Jewish priests who rejected and persecuted Jesus, the rich young ruler who went away from Jesus (Matthew 19:22), Ananias and Sapphira who died for a lie (Acts 5), and Peter confronted by Paul at Antioch for hypocrisy (Galatians 2:11).

Modern-day Christians are not immune from abominably poor choices. We've observed some who married inappropriately, became addicted to pornography or drugs, or lost their savings due to dubious financial decisions. These dramatic mistakes can damage a life. Less dramatic poor

2

choices also affect the quality of life. "How did we rack up so much credit card debt?" "I wish I had my old job back." "I should have eaten more healthy foods and exercised more."

Choice, not chance, determines destiny.[1] (Walk Thru the Bible Ministries)

Christians are not immune to poor corporate decisions as well. As groups, Christians have made many poor choices: the crusades, the Inquisition, the Thirty Years' War between Catholics and Protestants in which both sides committed unspeakable atrocities, witch trials, slavery in America, and racial apartheid (especially in the Bible Belt). Such choices dishonored God and discredited Him among non-believers. In current times, prominent Christians have made poor moral choices and thereby exposed all of Jesus' followers to charges of hypocrisy.

There is a whole genre of literature on effective decision-making, normally business oriented. They offer tips such as brainstorming alternatives, seeking diagnostic feedback, and visualizing outcomes. These are practical and can be useful. However, this mini-book is spiritually focused about how we can develop the ability to make good personal choices. Getting married? Looking for a different church? Changing jobs? Educating children? Caring for aging parents?

Drew: My mother sometimes said of different people, "He (or she) doesn't have a lick of sense." Her application was slightly different than saying a person didn't have any common sense. Although if phrases had relatives, "not a lick of sense" and "no common sense" would be

3

cousins. Common sense usually applies to knowledge, like how to use a can opener or the best way to build a campfire, whereas "not a lick of sense" applied to judgment: the ability to make good choices. Mom used the term to describe a young person who hung around the wrong crowd, someone who frittered away his money, or one who rebelled against authority just for the sake of rebelling.

We believe that God would have us to exercise sound judgment—that is to develop the sense or wisdom to make good choices. Even when the consequences of a choice aren't dire, each of us has limited time and energy. We need to make the best choices to optimize the life God has given to us.

Questions for Thought
What are some bad choices you've seen Christians make?

Have you observed consequences of bad choices?

How were others affected?

START WITH
THE PREMISE THAT
you are not wise

Do not be wise in your own estimation. (Romans 12:16)

Do not be wise in your own eyes. (Proverbs 3:7)

Many people make poor choices because they are overconfident in their own decision-making ability. A thorough study conducted by an international team through Max Plank Institute in Leipzig[2] and other studies have clearly shown that those who are less confident make a higher proportion of correct choices than those who are highly confident. Perhaps less confidence leads to more diligence in carefully assessing choices.

Solomon's Overconfidence

If anybody should have had confidence in his own wisdom, it was King Solomon. God offered a gift to the newly anointed king. "In that night God appeared to Solomon and said to him, 'Ask what I shall give you.' " (2 Chronicles 1:7) Solomon pleased God by asking for "wisdom and knowledge." Nine chapters of 2 Chronicles follow the story of Solomon's request for wisdom with his successes and the glories of his reign. After Solomon's wise response to the two women contending over a child, 1 Kings 3:28 says, "When all Israel heard of the judgment which the king had handed down, they feared the king, for they saw that the wisdom of God was in him to administer justice." 1 Kings 10:24 says, "All the earth was seeking the presence of Solomon, to hear his wisdom which God had put in his heart."

Solomon wrote about himself, "Behold, I have magnified and increased wisdom more than all who were over Jerusalem before me; and my mind has observed a wealth of wisdom and knowledge." (Ecclesiastes 1:16) And he said, "Then I became great and increased more than all who preceded me in Jerusalem. My wisdom also stood by me." (Ecclesiastes 2:9) Solomon was certainly confident in his wisdom.

Woe to those who are wise in their own eyes and clever in their own sight! (Isaiah 5:21)

1 Kings chapter 11 offers the second part of Solomon's story that probably resulted from overconfidence. Solomon's unwise relationships with foreign women led to dalliance with other gods. "Solomon did what was evil in the sight of the Lord, and did not follow the Lord fully, as David his father had done." (1 Kings 11:6) "Fully" is an interesting term knowing as we do about David's egregious sins. We interpret "fully"

in this context to mean that David did remain true to Yahweh versus other gods.

1 Kings 11:9-10 reports, "Now the Lord was angry with Solomon because his heart was turned away from the Lord, the God of Israel, who had appeared to him twice, and had commanded him concerning this thing, that he should not go after other gods; but he did not observe what the Lord had commanded." The result recorded in 1 Kings 11:11-12 was that God removed most of Israel from the authority of Solomon's descendants. The wisdom God initially gave to Solomon wasn't all-encompassing.

Questions for Thought

Have you observed individuals overconfident in their decision-making ability?

Were there consequences?

What are some possible reasons for overconfidence?

A Misleading Biblical Interpretation

But if any of you lacks wisdom, let him ask of God, who gives to all generously and without reproach, and it will be given to him. But he must ask in faith without any doubting, for the one who doubts is like the surf of the sea, driven and tossed by the wind. (James 1:5-6)

Asked about decision-making, many Bible-believing Christians would cite James 1:5-6. Their interpretation of that scripture would be that prior to deciding, a Christian need only to ask God without doubting, and the proper choice will be revealed. We believed this until we saw Christians relying on this interpretation and overconfidently making very ill-considered choices. We wish that good decision-making was that simple. It isn't. Romans 12:16 says, "Do not be wise in your own estimation." The NIV Bible translates verse sixteen as, "Do not be conceited." Misapplication of James 1:5-6 could lead to thinking oneself wise or becoming conceited through overconfidence in decision-making, like Solomon.

Please don't misunderstand. God can and does sometimes give sudden special insight in a situation.

Drew: I personally have received sudden insight on occasion, especially in tight situations. When we led a ministry in South Carolina, we were diligent to encompass a variety of Christian denominations by avoiding points of potential disagreement. Quite a few engineers with whom I worked were key volunteers helping us. One day a group of them, all dedicated Christians from different denominations, summoned me to join them in a theological debate. "Settle an issue for us," one said. "Can a saved person lose their salvation?" All of them waited expectantly for me to agree with their differing positions.

"What I believe is the parable of the sower," I began, hardly realizing what I was saying. "Some of the seed fell in good soil and yielded a great crop. Do those people go to heaven?" All the men nodded affirmation. "But some of the seed fell on rocky ground and dried up or among thorns and was choked out," I continued. Turning to the men whom I knew believed salvation could be lost I asked, "Were those people saved?" Those men indicated that those people were saved. "Then they lost it," I commented. Next, I turned to the men whom I knew believed salvation was irrevocable. "Were those people saved?" These men strongly indicated that those people had never been saved. "Then they didn't lose it." All the men were satisfied with that explanation, which revealed that their issue revolved around different usages of the word "saved."

That was the first time I had heard that

explanation myself. I believe God gave me instant wisdom when needed. I departed the group thanking God for a remarkable intervention to prevent me from taking sides among our volunteers. Later I suspected that Solomon's response to "divide the child" between two contending mothers was the same sort of intervention. This may be a parallel of Jesus' words in Matthew 10:19. "But when they hand you over, do not worry about how or what you are to say; for it will be given you in that hour what you are to say."

Although God sometimes grants special insight, we've also seen Christians rely on James 1:5-6 as a shortcut to easy wisdom. Carefully thinking a situation through and diligently collecting all available information is hard work. Even harder is long studying to have the background to make decisions in complex matters. Sadly, we've seen Christians use the easy wisdom interpretation of James 1:5-6 to even make medical or financial decisions they were poorly equipped to make.

Drew: I studied a lot in engineering school, hoping that high grades would lead to a good job. Then I became a follower of Christ and got involved in Christian activities on campus. My involvement kept me from doing my homework before an important exam. As the professor distributed the tests, I was terrified. "God, please save me!" I prayed. To my joy, the questions were just the things I knew. When I got my graded paper back with an A, I thought, "This is wonderful. Now that I'm a Christian, I won't need to study anymore."

I went back to my Christian activities. At the next exam, I wasn't worried. Matthew 21:22 promised, "If you believe, you will receive whatever you ask for in prayer."(NIV) I remember praying, "Okay, Lord, I'm believing and asking." Opening the exam, I learned that God is not a genie. He expected me to do my homework to learn the engineering principles necessary to make good engineering decisions.

Like Drew learned through this engineering school experience, we believe that the best interpretation of James 1:5-6 includes God expecting believers to do their homework in acquiring wisdom. Our interpretation is that we can be certain "without any doubting" that God will build wisdom over a lifetime into those who ask. Faith is required because wisdom does not come quickly or easily. God expects those seeking wisdom to do their homework through studying and accurately interpreting Scripture, evaluating their experiences, and understanding all the truth of His creation. Read through Proverbs where God admonishes us to seek after wisdom and understanding. We should not attempt to treat God like a genie.

Other observations also refute the easy wisdom interpretation of James 1:5-6. Notice that James does not put the promise of wisdom from God in the context of specific decisions. James even warns that some prayers are not answered. "You ask and do not receive, because you ask with wrong motives, so that you may spend it on your pleasures." (James 4:3) We have seen James 1:5-6 claimed with the wrong motive—the desire for a lazy shortcut to wisdom and understanding.

Why would Scripture extol the benefit of many counselors (Proverbs 15:22) if an individual could perfectly assess the best choice directly from God simply by "faith without any doubting"? We've been part of groups meeting to consider a course of action who sincerely prayed claiming James 1:5-6. At the prayer's conclusion, each person present had seemingly received different wisdom from God. Clearly God wasn't simply giving the best choice solely by our asking. If Christians could so easily summon wisdom from God, you would think they would be in demand as professional choice-makers.

> Sometimes we can assume we've walked with God so long that every "religious" thought we have is from Him. Untrue.[3] (Beth Moore)

Perhaps you've heard the saying, "Often wrong, but never in doubt." If you've known people like that, you've observed how difficult and unreasonable they can be. James 3:17

characterizes "wisdom from above" as "reasonable." The non-doubting, easy wisdom interpretation of James 1:5-6 contributes to those who might be unreasonable and overconfident. In the extreme, some think they are channeling God. We once heard a director in a Christian organization confidently claim that he never made a mistake. We personally saw him make several grievous mistakes and fail to acknowledge them. He had become overconfident in himself and failed to exercise sound judgment.

> *For through the grace given to me I say to everyone among you not to think more highly of himself than he ought to think; but to think so as to have sound judgment, as God has allotted to each a measure of faith. (Romans 12:3)*

Questions for Thought

What do you think of the interpretation of James 1:5-6 as a means of easy wisdom?

Have you observed ways that Christians sometimes treat God like a genie?

Have you ever been given special insight from God in a situation?

Acquiring Wisdom and Understanding

Acquire wisdom! Acquire understanding! Do not forget nor turn away from the words of my mouth. Do not forsake her, and she will guard you; Love her, and she will watch over you. The beginning of wisdom is: Acquire wisdom; And with all your acquiring, get understanding. Prize her, and she will exalt you; She will honor you if you embrace her. She will place on your head a garland of grace; She will present you with a crown of beauty. Hear, my son, and accept my sayings and the years of your life will be many. I have directed you in the way of wisdom; I have led you in upright paths. When you walk, your steps will not be impeded; And if you run, you will not stumble. Take hold of instruction; do not let go. Guard her, for she is your life. (Proverbs 4:5-13)

The Child [Jesus] continued to grow and become strong, increasing in wisdom; and the grace of God was upon Him. (Luke 2:40)

Although considering ourselves wise is folly, we can increase in wisdom and understanding. David prayed, "Teach me good discernment and knowledge, For I believe in Your commandments." (Psalm 119:66) Much of Proverbs is about seeking wisdom and understanding. Even Jesus increased in wisdom over time according to Luke 2:40. But we need to remember Solomon and not get overconfident. Let us maintain in our hearts, *I am not wise. I do not have all the answers. But I thank God that I have increased in wisdom over time.*

Questions for Thought

Why do you think increasing in wisdom is important?

What are some reasons individuals might not seek to increase in wisdom?

How can people deceive themselves that they are wise?

What are some ways to develop wisdom?

WORLDLY
wisdom

For the wisdom of this world is foolishness before God. (1 Corinthians 3:19)

Who among you is wise and understanding? Let him show by his good behavior his deeds in the gentleness of wisdom. But if you have bitter jealousy and selfish ambition in your heart, do not be arrogant and so lie against the truth. This wisdom is not that which comes down from above, but is earthly, natural, demonic. For where jealousy and selfish ambition exist, there is disorder and every evil thing. But the wisdom from above is first pure, then peaceable, gentle, reasonable, full of mercy and good fruits, unwavering, without hypocrisy. And the seed whose fruit is righteousness is sown in peace by those who make peace. (James 3:13-18)

Clearly the Bible draws a distinction between worldly wisdom and wisdom from God. We believe that wisdom from God, for which He usually requires us to do our homework, leads to good choices and the best decisions. Let us begin to discover the route to good decisions by identifying how bad decisions can be made through worldly wisdom.

"Always Follow Your Heart"

A frequent theme in romantic fiction usually oriented toward women is "Always follow your heart." Men have found an alternative method to express the same sentiment: "Go with your gut." And there is some truth to these sayings. A few people are gifted in intuition. They can pick up on hidden clues that can give insight not apparent to others. The old Celtic peoples attributed the gift to the supernatural and described the person as "fey."

However, the Bible warns, "The heart is more deceitful than all else and is desperately sick; who can understand it?" (Jeremiah 17:9) The old King James translation calls our hearts "desperately wicked." History also shows that human hearts are superstitious. Humans have always made up things to explain what they couldn't understand. The Bible doesn't use the mostly male word "gut." But both heart and gut refer to an instinct within our sinful nature.

Our hearts, or our gut, are connected to our emotions. Anger, fear, longing, or other emotions can distort judgment. Those who ascribe to the overly simplistic interpretation of James 1:5-6 can easily misinterpret their emotions as wisdom from God. Notice again that James' description of "wisdom from above" in James 3:17 includes the qualifier "reasonable." Acting on emotion is not reasonable.

18

The people of Israel during the period following their conquest of the Promised Land had God's law. They had the presence of God in the Ark of the Covenant. They had memories and monuments to the works God had done. And yet, a recurring theme in the book of Judges is "Every man did what was right in his own eyes." the result was turmoil and frequent subjugation to foreign powers. They let their hearts and guts determine their decisions. Samson, for example, let his love and pursuit of Delilah blind him to her tricks, which resulted in his downfall.

Drew: My widowed mother had a unique concept of justice. She considered punishing the innocent preferable to letting the guilty escape. Therefore, whenever something happened and her three children each denied responsibility, she punished all of us. As the oldest, I got the worst. As you might expect, that resulted in some anger.

One such occasion of unjust punishment occurred on the day the family was going to the county fair. Aside from Christmas, the county fair was perhaps the highlight of our year. Fuming at the injustice, my heart told me to boycott the fair in protest. But my head said, "You're justified, but who will be the loser? Don't miss the fair because you're mad." I did choose to go to the fair and had a wonderful time with my family. Afterwards, I rejoiced in that choice. And I purposed to not let my emotions control my choices.

Questions for Thought

Have you observed individuals follow their heart or gut into trouble? Can you give examples?

Can we trust our emotions? Why or why not?

"No Time Like the Present"

And He said, "A man had two sons. The younger of them said to his father, 'Father, give me the share of the estate that falls to me.' So he divided his wealth between them. And not many days later, the younger son gathered everything together and went on a journey into a distant country, and there he squandered his estate with loose living. Now when he had spent everything, a severe famine occurred in that country, and he began to be impoverished. So he went and hired himself out to one of the citizens of that country, and he sent him into his fields to feed swine. And he would have gladly filled his stomach with the pods that the swine were eating, and no one was giving anything to him. But when he came to his senses, he said, 'How many of my father's hired men have more than enough bread, but I am dying here with hunger!' " (Luke 15:11-17)

Jesus went on to tell about the father receiving his younger son with joy. The parable of the prodigal son is a beautiful and unforgettable picture of God our father extending forgiveness and love to even the worst offender. However, the story does not minimize the consequences of the younger son's poor choice. Later the father says to his older son, "all that is mine is yours." (Luke 15:31) The father did not redistribute the inheritance. The younger son had squandered his inheritance seeking instant gratification.

Beth Moore describes people as "trained by our culture to have a severe allergy to delayed gratification and the attention span of a fruit fly."[4] Drew shares a story in the companion mini-book, *More Than Ordinary Wisdom*, about his last days of freedom before leaving home for college. He pursued a large fish on an idyllic river all summer. The climax of the story taught him a powerful lesson.

Near dark in the chilly December twilight, I went down to the river bank. Mostly I wanted to feel the rod in my hands and hear the water. These were the last casts in the last days of boyhood. The only spot with enough light remaining to cast was where I had never seen fish before. To my surprise, a big fish grabbed the lure. After a minute of tussle, the smallmouth was in my hands.

Eating it immediately came to my mind. Then a voice in my head said, *Let this one go. For the rest of your life, you can enjoy the thought of this fish and its descendants alive and free in this river.* But, youthful passions being what they are, the thought of tasting its sweet flesh was too much to give up. I killed, cooked, and ate the smallmouth. Before the dishes were cleaned, I felt sorrow. My worthy adversary was gone forever. For a moment of pleasure, I had taken on a lifetime of regret.

One fish is a small price for a teenager to learn such a powerful lesson before leaving home for college and an adventurous life. The wisdom to make careful decisions is worth any fish. That fish helped to make me who I am. For those reasons, I no longer regret eating the smallmouth. Still, it would be wonderful to think of the smallmouth's descendants living in the river.[5] (Coons, *More Than Ordinary Wisdom*)

The principle of delayed gratification is one in which a person forgoes a premature pleasure in favor of greater satisfaction or success later. Walter Mischel, a professor at Stanford University, conducted a series of studies on delayed gratification.[6] The famous "marshmallow experiment" offered children a choice between one marshmallow, cookie, or pretzel, or two of the same if they waited for 15 minutes. In follow-up studies, the researchers found that children who were able to wait longer for the preferred rewards tended to have better life outcomes.

"I must have it now!" is the battle cry of those who refuse to delay self-gratification. Oswald Chambers says that is the essential definition of lust—the belief that it is my right to have what I want when I want it. Couple the inability to delay gratification with the availability of everything we want or need, and match that with the painless purchasing plan of credit cards, and it is no wonder that the average American family now carries more than $9,000 in credit card debt.[7] (Zig Ziglar)

James 1:4 says, "And let endurance have its perfect result, so that you may be perfect and complete, lacking in nothing." The instantaneous genie-like interpretation of receiving wisdom sometimes taken from verses 5-6 may be caused by a desire for instant gratification. Wisdom usually requires endurance.

Questions for Thought

What are some ways people insist on instant gratification to their long-term detriment?

How can that limit their future?

"Never Admit a Mistake"

But because of your stubbornness and unrepentant heart you are storing up wrath for yourself in the day of wrath and revelation of the righteous judgment of God. (Romans 2:5)

Persistence can be a virtue. However, when persistence becomes stubbornness, making good choices becomes difficult. Paul admonished the Romans for their failure to choose God's ways.

The term "unrepentant heart" particularly stands out. A person holding on to a bad choice rather than change compounds the bad choice. Since nearly all people want others to think well of them, many are unwilling to admit a mistake or even acknowledge it to themselves.

A Christian organization placed the employee-funded 403(b) retirement plans of individuals into a small non-fiduciary investing company. They lost everyone's individual savings. The chilling thing was when we heard people say, "God must have wanted us to lose that money." If so, apparently God didn't want those who invested in more reputable companies to lose their money.

"Sunk cost" is a term to describe the human reluctance to change directions when time, money, or effort has already been expended in an endeavor. People are extremely reluctant to admit or accept that loss when circumstances change or new information is available.

Drew: I once lost a lot of money on a single equity investment. Prior to purchasing the stock, I had done the things usually needed for a good decision—research: the federally required financial statement looked good; prior decision: the company fit the profile I like of dull dividend-payers; and counselors: three professional rating services gave them a "strong buy"; none gave them a "sell." Then in one day the stock plunged 80%. Federal agents had raided my stock's company headquarters about inaccurate financial statements.

I held on, desperately hoping that it was a

misunderstanding, and thereby lost more money. Finally, my financial adviser demanded, "Why do you still own that? Would you buy it now for the listed price?" The truth was that I just couldn't accept the loss. I admitted letting sunk cost dictate my decision. Then I sold the stock. With the remaining money, I bought something that made a good profit. Fortunately, diversification had limited our loss to only a year of living expenses.

Sometimes people have invested years of their lives into an endeavor that isn't going well. We once led a marriage seminar for couples all older than ourselves. Usually at the end of a seminar, young couples cluster around us asking questions and sharing experiences, frequently for an hour or more. Not the older audience. They stampeded out of the meeting place. In less than one minute, we stood completely alone. We believe the couples realized the truth of the biblical principles we shared. But having invested a lifetime in doing things the wrong way, the thought of changing frightened them away.

Sometimes we have started a project only to realize that the required work would be much more that we had anticipated. The question to ask ourselves is, "Regardless of the work already done, is this project worth the remaining work needed?" If not, then the best choice is to terminate the project and invest our energy elsewhere.

Kit: Drew and I have always enjoyed visiting farmers' markets. I had wanted to try having a stall when a new market opened in our town. Drew grew vegetables and I baked various breads and other goods. People taking our vegetables and baked goods home to serve their families was a joy. But with each new year more of my time revolved around getting ready for the weekly market. As springtime approached of our fourth year, we evaluated our choices and decided not to continue. Going to market was a dream I had wanted to try and am glad I did. While I missed not being at the market and my customers missed me, we discovered my time could be spent more productively. I believe our writing projects will have a more lasting influence.

Questions for Thought

Have you met people who refused to admit a mistake to others? To themselves?

How can this quality affect relationships?

When should you accept a mistake and move on?

THE IMPORTANCE OF
counselors

Without consultation, plans are frustrated. But with many counselors they succeed. (Proverbs 15:22)

When an engineer designs a part, he or she draws it from different viewpoints so that the machinist can see all the features that might be hidden by a single view. Counselors are valuable because they see an issue from different viewpoints. Counselors can also visualize alternatives we may not have considered. However, picking the right counselors is an important choice itself.

The Right Counselors

First, we favor counselors who are experts in certain fields and may have knowledge or tools that can clarify the issue. For example, if you are sick, go to a physician. Don't gather a group of friends and ask their diagnosis. Experts aren't always right. But guessers are nearly always wrong.

Next, put your spouse at the top of your list of potential counselors. Your spouse may not be an expert in medicine, finance, careers, relationships . . . or many other things. But they likely are an expert in one very important area: you. Your spouse is likely to know that the new boat looking so good in the showroom will likely only get used once a year. Or that cute puppy will soon grow into a large, neglected dog. In this regard, others who know you well—parents, siblings, and close friends—can also make highly qualified counselors.

> "We are soooo different," many couples have said to us. To which we reply, "Good. The more different you are, the more strengths you have as a team." God accentuated our differences by making us male and female. Plus, everyone has special talents and abilities.[8] (Coons, *More Than Ordinary Marriage*)

We advise that only in the rarest of circumstances should you unilaterally make a choice to which your spouse objects. God made men and women different by design. One purpose is that they almost always see issues from different angles. Keep talking to each other. Look for other alternatives. Weigh how strongly the other feels. When we have a disagreement about a choice, and one of us favors one alternative strongly whereas the other favors his or her opinion mildly, we go with the stronger opinion. Also recognize when emotions might overly influence either of you.

Kit: I suffered medical issues as a teenager and fear hospitals and doctors. On one occasion after we were married, I felt sick and developed a high fever. Drew strongly suggested seeing a doctor. Although fearful, I put faith in Drew's judgment. The doctor discovered a severe infection in my only kidney. They rushed me to the hospital where they began immediate treatment. Had the infection persisted, I could have lost the kidney and needed dialysis.

Finally, search for counselors who have a strong record of ethical behavior. Note that worldly success does not necessarily make someone a qualified counselor. Many people, unencumbered by ethics, prosper.

Jeremiah expressed his concern, "Righteous are You, O Lord, that I would plead my case with You; Indeed I would discuss matters of justice with You: Why has the way of the wicked prospered? Why are all those who deal in treachery at ease?" (Jeremiah 12:1)

David said not to fret because of them. "Rest in the Lord and wait patiently for Him; Do not fret because of him who prospers in his way, because of the man who carries out wicked schemes." (Psalm 37:7)

Job rejected them from being his counselors. "Behold, their prosperity is not in their hand; The counsel of the wicked is far from me. (Job 21:16)

Questions for Thought
Where can a person find good counselors?

29

Have you observed people who appeared to prosper through doing wrong?

The Wrong Counselors

Beware of the false prophets, who come to you in sheep's clothing, but inwardly are ravenous wolves. (Matthew 7:15)

Drew: Prior to the 2008-9 "Great Recession," I smelled trouble coming in the financial markets. But what to do? In preparation, I read about fifty books on finances and investing. I learned one thing: no matter what lame-brained thing you want to do with your savings, some financial "expert" will endorse it and offer to help you for a commission. Statistics prove that 80% of investment-fund managers perform worse than the Standard and Poor's 500 index. That means that you will average better returns trusting a monkey with a dartboard to pick your stocks. The probable reason is that professional investors are willing to take great risks with your money. If they can luck into a stellar year, new clients will flock to the latest hot picker. They can make a lot of money before the averages catch up with them.

A wise man seeks much counsel . . . a fool listens to all of it.[9] (Larry Burkett)

In the same manner that you can receive any financial advice you desire, religious experts are available to confirm virtually anything you want to believe. Recently, *USA Today*[10] and numerous other news outlets reported that Unification Sanctuary, a church in Pennsylvania, held a "gun blessing" service for the AR-15 automatic rifle used in several recent mass killings. The church believes that the "rod of iron" associated with Jesus in Revelation 12:5 and 19:5 is the AR-15.

The New Testament has a lot to say about false teachers. Jesus, Paul, Peter, John, and Jude all warned about false teachers. But what is a false teacher? John gave a criterion in 1 John 4:1 and 2 John 7. The false teacher would not confess that Jesus Christ had come in the flesh. A few biblically defined false teachers are around in various cults. But most 21st century religious groups have excluded false teachers as defined by John.

However, perhaps a more pertinent warning is Paul's writing to Timothy, "For the time will come when they will not endure sound doctrine; but wanting to have their ears tickled, they will accumulate for themselves teachers in accordance to their own desires." (2 Timothy 4:3)

Plenty of Bible teachers who would not deny Christ in the flesh are inaccurate in their teaching. A few are simply charlatans taking advantage of people for personal gain. We hear religious broadcasters promise God's favor in return for donations, frequently linking the degree of favor to the size of donation. At the core, this is the same as the discredited practice of selling indulgences. Most of the other inaccurate teachers believe the inaccuracies they proclaim. They have been misled by others or are self-deceived.

There is no lie as sly as the one we tell ourselves.[11] (Beth Moore)

Drew: In the 1970s, eschatology, or end times teaching, was popular. The formation of the Jewish state of Israel in Palestine by the UN in 1948 following the Balfour Declaration of 1917 signaled to many the imminence of the return of Christ. In Matthew 24 Jesus had told about the end times and concluded that after signs, "Truly I say to you, this generation will not pass away until all these things take place."

A generation was roughly forty years by the example of the Hebrews who wandered in the desert. Therefore, eschatologists claimed that although nobody knew the exact date, Jesus would return about 1988 or before. Having heard this from my pastor and other supposedly biblical experts, I taught this to my Sunday school class. It wasn't true. I didn't mean to teach untruth. I just repeated what I had heard without real understanding.

Many people lead us into deception because they themselves are deceived.[12] (Beth Moore)

American Christian culture is largely a competitive consumer culture. If people don't hear what they want from their pastor or other teacher, plenty of other churches or groups beckon. Ear ticklers can draw large niche audiences by telling people what they want to hear. Personal preference is one reason that there are so many variations in Christian teaching. Large audiences in the Christian world are interpreted as a sign of God's favor. Others emulate that method of ear tickling. And Christian understanding of God's truth is thereby contaminated.

People also want certainty. We once had a pastor who was growing in wisdom. In his sermons, he would sometimes say, "I haven't fully figured out this scripture. It could mean this. Or it could mean that." We liked, respected, and trusted him. We appreciated that he was searching for the best possible interpretation rather than simply repeating what others had said. He didn't last at that church, though. Most people already knew what they wanted to believe and expected their pastor to confirm it.

For the best decision-making based on the Bible, we need to be careful whom we listen to. Even sincere Christian leaders can mislead us. We suggest starting with this assumption: nobody is perfect in wisdom. Apostle Paul wrote, "For now we see in a mirror dimly." (1 Corinthians 13:12) Mirrors in those days were hand-polished metal, mostly brass, rather than the highly reflective mirrors we use today. Those mirrors distorted the image. Paul communicated that our understanding is not complete. The best voices to listen to are those who truly know that their understanding is incomplete and are increasing in their own wisdom. They are open to deeper understanding of Scripture and can change their own minds.

Drew: Kit and I once had lunch along with several others with a famous Christian speaker and writer. During our meal, he espoused a popular Christian philosophy that I had once believed myself. I respectfully shared some historical facts and quoted several scriptures. The man sat for a moment considering my arguments. Suddenly he said, "You're right." He continued speaking to himself, "We've been wrong about that." I would listen to that man again.

By contrast, we heard the president of a seminary use a rhetorical trick to discredit those with different values than his own. When I pointed out the trick and distortion, he refused to discuss it or even respond. I would have been willing to be proved wrong for my own improvement. But he was simply self-assured and closed-minded. I would not listen to that man again.

Questions for Thought

What are some qualities to watch out for in likely wrong counselors?

Why do so many people select the wrong counselors?

GOD'S WORD CORRECTLY INTERPRETED LEADS TO THE
best choices

How can a young man keep his way pure? By keeping it according to Your word. With all my heart I have sought You; Do not let me wander from Your commandments. Your word I have treasured in my heart, that I may not sin against You. (Psalm 119:9–11)

Your word is a lamp to my feet and a light to my path. (Psalm 119:105)

The Bible is our best source for making the right decisions. Most of God's will for our lives is contained in Scripture. The Bible teaches us sins to avoid that can hurt us, even ruin our lives.

Sin is serious business to God. Much of the hardship in people's lives is unnecessary. It could be avoided by following God's instructions.[13] (Coons, *More Than Ordinary Faith*)

Do not be deceived, God is not mocked; for whatever
a man sows, this he will also reap. For the one who
sows to his own flesh will from the flesh reap corruption.
(Galatians 6:7-8)

Choices Before a Crisis

The Bible helps us to make choices before they are needed. When Moses led the children of Israel out of Egypt toward the Promised Land, they stopped to camp on the banks of the Jordan River. There they chose twelve men to spy out the land. The spies spent 40 days and nights across the river and returned to report: "We went in to the land where you sent us; and it certainly does flow with milk and honey, and this is its fruit." (Numbers 13:27) But they also reported that there were giants in the land, and fortified cities that would be impossible to conquer. Joshua and Caleb among the spies knew better — the land could be conquered because God was with them.

Yet fear made the people side with the majority report and refuse to enter the land. As a result, God decreed that the people would wander in the desert for 40 years, one year for each day the spies had been in the land. Forty years later, Joshua led the children of Israel back to the banks of the Jordan. Without pausing for debate, they waded into the river and entered the Promised Land. Because that choice had been made in advance, their emotions of fear did not sway them.

Drew: My pastor's wife used to warn, "You shouldn't wait until you're in the backseat of a car to decide not to have sex." She was right. But the principle is much broader than sex. The Bible can help us make decisions about various temptations before the emotions of the moment lead us astray.

Questions for Thought
Why should some decisions be made in advance?

What are some decisions that should be made in advance based on God's Word?

Danger in Misunderstanding the Bible

Just as also our beloved brother Paul, according to the wisdom given him, wrote to you, as also in all his letters, speaking in them of these things, in which are some things hard to understand, which the untaught and unstable distort, as they do also the rest of the Scriptures, to their own destruction. (2 Peter 3:15-16)

Because, as Peter says, the Bible can be hard to understand or distorted, we must work hard to discover correct interpretations of Scripture. An incorrect interpretation of Scripture can lead to bad choices. Many men and women have died from venomous snake bites during Christian church services. They literally apply Mark 16:17-18 ("they will pick up serpents") from the King James Bible translated from Latin manuscripts. Some snake handlers' interpretation is so certain that they refuse treatment when bitten and continue the practice even after being bitten, even though family members have previously died from being bitten. Biblical scholars report that the oldest Greek texts of Scripture do not contain the passage used to justify handling snakes. Some might contend, "God wouldn't allow Scripture to be distorted." But according to 2 Peter 3:15-16, God does.

> It isn't what we don't know that gives us trouble, it's what we know that ain't so. (Will Rogers)

Martin Luther, an early-16th-century monk of the Augustinian order and later theology professor in Wittenberg, Germany, challenged the biblical interpretations of the established church. His writings formed the foundation of the Reformation. Although generally hailed as the beginning of Protestantism, his ideas ultimately reformed the Catholic Church as well, particularly in the issue of selling indulgences. We are not Martin Luther. But we can and should examine and purify what we believe. An accurate interpretation of Scripture can stand scrutiny.

Cultural Bias in Interpretation

Randy Richards served as a Christian missionary in Indonesia. In a remarkable book, *Misreading Scripture with Western*

Eyes—Removing Cultural Blinders to Better Understand the Bible, he has revealed many ways that American culture has biased our interpretation of Scripture.

We can easily forget that Scripture is a foreign land and that reading the Bible is a cross cultural experience. To open the Word of God is to step into a strange world where things are very unlike our own. Most of us don't speak the languages. We don't know geography or the customs or what behaviors are considered rude or polite. And yet we hardly notice. For many of us, the Bible is more familiar than any other book. We may have parts of it memorized. And because we believe that the Bible is God's Word to us, no matter where on the planet or when in history we read it, we tend to read Scripture in our own *when* and *where*, in a way that makes sense on our terms.

As we will see, it is a better method to speak of what the passage meant to the original hearers, and then to ask how that applies to us. Another way to say this is that all Bible reading is necessarily contextual. There is no purely objective interpretation. This is not postmodern relativism. We believe truth is truth. But there's no way around the fact that our cultural and historical contexts supply us with habits of mind that lead us to read the Bible differently than Christians in other cultural and historical contexts.[14] (Randy Richards)

Martin Luther serves also as an example of allowing cultural bias to creep into belief. After having made such a courageous stand for biblical truth, he publicly expressed strong antagonistic views towards Jews. Among other persecutions, Luther suggested that Jewish synagogues and schools be burned, homes of Jews be destroyed, their money confiscated, rabbis threatened with death, and Jews not be allowed to travel[15] — chilling sentiments used to justify German atrocities in later centuries. Martin Luther should serve as a reminder that any of us can err.

Personal Bias in Interpretation

Honest Bible teachers will admit, "You can make the Bible say anything you want." We Christians sometimes inappropriately pick verses to justify what we want to think. Theologians are aware of the problem of biblical misinterpretation. "Eisegesis" is the word used to describe a process by which personal presuppositions, agendas, or biases are superimposed onto Scripture. This is a temptation for anyone who reads and attempts to apply Scripture. The challenge is to recognize that temptation and to fight against it.

God's Word is never wrong. But our interpretation can be wrong. Some may protest, "But the Holy Spirit wouldn't allow that." To this we respond, "Why then are there so many different interpretations from different denominations and types of Christians?" History also proves that well-meaning Christians can get things very wrong. Galileo was put on trial for heresy after asserting that the earth revolved around the sun.

Finding the Most Accurate Interpretation

Many resources give guidelines for the correct interpretation of Scripture. They talk about such things as the support of other passages, context, historical interpretations, and the Holy Spirit. All good. We've yet to see an interpretational guideline that included, "Give it a reality check. Look at the evidence supporting or refuting an interpretation." Jesus, when answering his critics said, "But wisdom is proved right by her deeds." (Matthew 11:19, NIV) This means examining the results of various teachings. Our James 1:5-6 analysis provides an example of our attempting to do so. Many snake handlers would have lived had they evaluated their biblical interpretation based on the results.

> He then answered, "Whether He is a sinner, I do not know; one thing I do know, that though I was blind, now I see." (John 9:25)

> "If this man were not from God, He could do nothing." (John 9:33)

John chapter 9 tells the story of Jesus healing a blind beggar. Afterwards the Pharisees concluded that Jesus had sinned by healing the man on the Sabbath. Their exchange with the healed man is comical. He asserted the obvious evidence of a miracle and concluded that Jesus was from God. They held onto their dogma despite the reality in front of them. They were willfully spiritually blind.

Remember my student homework experience? Evidence showed that my biblical interpretation, influenced by self-interest, wasn't accurate. 1 Thessalonians 5:21 specifically relating to wisdom from God says, "But examine everything carefully; hold fast to that which is good." Especially when there are conflicting biblical interpretations within the church, we should look for evidence to verify or deny. The Bible is always true. But our interpretations often are inaccurate and lead to bad choices.

Drew: I once observed a con man take money from Bible-believing Christians. I warned them that the inflated promises, secrecy, and story inconsistencies evidenced fraud. But wanting to believe the con man's promises, they ignored the evidence, interpreted Scripture accordingly, and went ahead. Many thousands of dollars were lost.

When is the last time you changed your mind about something? People who never change their minds have stopped growing. Understanding Scripture more deeply frequently requires changing our minds. Questioning our own assumptions and looking at facts both biblical and non-biblical can lead to better understanding and choices.

There is a remarkable, albeit not well-known, story in Acts 10. Before that time Peter and the other apostles considered the message of Christ just for the Jewish people. Their understanding of the law of Moses and scriptures justified that. Then when they saw the Gentiles receiving the gift of the Holy Spirit, they could not deny the fact that Jesus' message was for all people. "Opening his mouth Peter said, 'I most certainly understand now that God is not one to show partiality.' " (Acts 10:34) Peter's observations of reality forced him to change his interpretation of Scripture.

Questions for Thought

How could misinterpretation of Scripture lead to poor choices?

Have you heard Bible teachers pulling meaning from Scripture that you doubted?

When was the last time that you changed your mind about a meaning of Scripture?

ALL TRUTH IS
God's truth

———

"All truth is God's truth." Although a cliché, this is accurate. Spiritual truth, scientific truth, mathematical truth, and historical truth cannot contradict each other because all belong to God. The great theologian Augustine compared secular truth to the valuable gold and silver the Israelites took out of pagan Egypt. Augustine taught churchmen to appropriate God's valuable truth from any source. All of God's truth is useful in making wise choices.[16] We believe Christianity should be about the truth, beginning with Jesus' "I am the way, and the truth, and the life; no one comes to the Father but through Me," (John 14:6) but not ending there.

Jesus said, "At least believe on the evidence of the works themselves." (John 14:11, NIV) God has provided plenty of evidence for faith within the universe scientists investigate. For example, behavioral scientists have shown that anger, hatred, and even poor neighbor relations are bad for our health. Jesus, who taught principles for our well-being, warned against these 2,000 years ago. According to the big bang theory, everything suddenly appeared from nothing. Does this not shout out "God"? Interestingly, the big bang was first recognized in 1927 by MIT-educated Georges Lemaitre, an ordained priest.

More recently, extremists among both scientists and churchmen have given each group ample reasons for distrust of the other. Richards Dawkins, an atheist biologist and frequent talk show guest, regularly attacks Christianity with acerbic wit, supposedly on behalf of science. Celebrity scientists Stephen Hawking, Carl Sagan, and others publicly rejected God. Science can rely on extraordinarily complex mathematics, which yield non-intuitive answers. Results reported by scientists are therefore impossible for non-scientists to verify and can even vary over time. Medical researchers, for example, can't seem to settle on whether certain foods are good or bad for our health. No wonder churchmen can be skeptical of science.

Scientists observe that there are conflicting beliefs within the church. Churchmen who claim to get unsubstantiated messages directly from God make scientists scoff. A few within the church are hostile to science even to the point of refusing medical care for their children. Some scientists fear that religion could undo scientific advancements that have saved lives and improved living conditions.

Both churchmen and scientists seek God's truth. And each can learn from the other. Romans 12:16 admonishes, "Live in harmony with one another." (NIV) Let us not allow different methodologies or extremists to cause us to disregard all the truthful evidence. Faith in combination with facts can help us make wise choices. Believers don't need to fear or reject "secular" truth in favor of a decision that outwardly seems more spiritual. The best choices are made by using all of God's truth. And all truth is God's truth.

Objectively Evaluate Alternatives

For God has not given us a spirit of timidity, but of power and love and sound judgment. (2 Timothy 1:7)

All the secular sources for decision-making emphasize using sound judgment to objectively evaluate each of the alternatives before choosing. Admittedly, being objective can be difficult. Counselors can help to do that, although they bring their own biases to the discussion. Looking at evidence as if it's being presented in a court can add objectivity. Considering WWJD — What Would Jesus Do — can also add objectivity.

In applying sound judgment, remember that God nearly always follows His own natural laws. He has suspended the law of gravity to part the Red Sea and overrode principles of biology to miraculously heal people. But almost always, God follows His own natural laws. Reading through the life of Abraham in Genesis chapters 12-25, miracle seems to follow miracle. But Abraham lived for 175 years. In that context, miracles weren't that frequent even in the life of God's chosen patriarch.

The mathematics of probability are part of God's natural laws. He nearly always follows them.

Drew: I believe in miracles. And I'm grateful to have witnessed a very few. The Christian organization Kit and

47

I served had a potentially major donor for my area, Eastern Europe and Russia. Three different managers had talked to the donor with no results. "Let me talk to them," I suggested. They refused and would tell me neither the donor's name nor location.

A major event in St. Petersburg, Russia, had been planned. Someone uninvolved suggested that we discover the American sister-city of St. Petersburg and invite somebody from that city to accompany us. Although I didn't see any merit to that idea, I wanted to be polite. I asked my administrative assistant to research the sister-city, find the name of a volunteer there, ask for the name of a Christian in the city, then call the Christian and invite them to join us to represent their city. A few days later she told me she had found a couple willing to go and gave me a name neither of us had ever heard before.

The next morning, the director of Donor Development came to my desk. "I understand you invited our potential donor to Russia," he said with irritation in his voice. The couple my administrative assistant had unknowingly invited was the one they had refused to let me challenge. On the trip, I gave them a proposal. The couple donated several hundred thousand dollars to our project. The probability that this was not a miracle is remote.

However, God rarely overrules natural laws, including those of probability. Therefore, appreciating the secular science of probability and using it to objectively evaluate alternatives helps us to make wise choices. Physicians—who must make good choices on behalf of their patients—rely heavily on statistics and probability.

Avoid Acting Rashly

Secular sources for decision-making recommend taking plenty of time to make the best choice. The biggest mistakes are made when people act rashly, perhaps in difficult circumstances. We've seen people quit their jobs over an injustice or slight without an alternate means to provide for their families.

We use a word picture: "Don't throw yourself in the water." The word picture evokes a vision of a ship sinking. Jumping into the water prematurely is not wise. Perhaps a rescue boat will appear if you simply wait. Or you may fashion a flotation device. At the very least, you'll conserve your strength until absolutely needed.

Drew: Twenty-five years ago, I worked as an engineer. As part of a team management system, I became the engineering liaison to the marketing department. There I had access to the pricing structure and testing results *for our products and our competitors'. I realized that the ship of our division was slowly sinking without a competitive advantage. I worked hard to keep us afloat, but at the same time started preparing a lifeboat of a job alternative. Five years later Kit and I were able to transition to that lifeboat, which offered a lot of exciting opportunities to serve God. And a couple of years later, the division did fail.*

Our mini-book *More Than Ordinary Challenges: Dealing with the Unexpected* includes a section about how to avoid making a difficult situation worse. In the Bible, Sarai knew about God's promise of a child to Abraham. But she acted rashly by giving her maid to her husband.

> Sarai had tired of waiting and felt compelled to do something about the situation. Admittedly Abram wasn't much help. But Sarai only made things worse—worse for her, worse for Abram, and worse for Hagar.[17] (Coons, *More Than Ordinary Challenges*)

Remember the section about making decisions ahead of when they are needed. Building in some safeguards can help you to avoid making rash decisions. Not making a major decision over your spouse's objections is a good safeguard. Although this sounds trivial, we have a family rule to pass on any major purchases that come with, "This offer is good only today." That safeguard has saved us from financial decisions we would have regretted later.

Take Some Chances

The Powerball lottery is a cultural phenomenon. Television shows lines of people waiting to spend their hard-earned money on chances to win hundreds of millions of dollars. Someone has said, "Powerball is a tax on people who are bad in math." But people aren't dumb. They know that one chance in 292,201,338 is essentially no chance. Many humorous comparisons give reality to the nearly impossible odds. Our favorite is that a person is four times more likely to be killed by an asteroid than to win the Powerball jackpot. And yet people flock to the lottery in droves. Why? They are purchasing a small whiff of hope. For a brief moment before the numbers are drawn, people can imagine themselves becoming unimaginably wealthy.

However, making good choices should be about more than hoping for an unlikely result. Life involves chances. Every time you get in a car, you are taking a chance of injury. Making good choices involves developing the wisdom to weigh the chance versus the reward or the potential consequences. For example, putting on a seatbelt takes a few seconds in the unlikelihood of an accident. But the consequences of an un-belted accident are severe. And over the course of a lifetime riding in cars, most people will need a seatbelt at some time. Putting on a seatbelt is a good choice.

Risks do not mean testing God. In the wilderness, Satan attempted to tempt Jesus. "And Jesus answered and said to him, 'It is said, You shall not put the Lord your God to the test.' " (Luke 4:12) We should not test God with a foolish risk. Any activity that requires God's intervention to avoid a catastrophe is testing Him. For example, putting your family's savings into a dubious investment by faith and expecting God to provide a high return. Violating moral principles and expecting God to work the situation for our good tests Him.

Nevertheless, taking risks is frequently essential for success. Failures will not stop you from ultimately succeeding. But fear of failure will stop you from succeeding. The issue is whether the risk is worth taking. A rough understanding of the mathematics of probability can help you discern when the odds and rewards are in your favor. Let God decide when to intervene with a miracle by suspending the laws of probability. In the meantime, we should use the sound judgment promised in 2 Timothy 1:7.

Questions for Thought

What do you think about St. Augustine's admonition to use secular truth?

What are some ways to help our objectivity in evaluating alternatives before making a choice?

Do you have any safeguards to help prevent you from acting rashly?

How do you determine whether a chance is worth taking?

BEWARE OF SECOND-GUESSING
yourself

___

In fifty years of Christian ministry, we have met many people with regrets. Some try to cope by justifying poor choices. For example, an impoverished single mother might point to a child and say something like, "If I hadn't slept with that bum, I wouldn't have little Jeffery." The implication is that God orchestrated the poor choice that contributed to her poverty. As explained in our mini-book *More Than Ordinary Faith*, we believe the best interpretation of Romans 8:28 is good for mankind and not always the individual in this life. However, we stoutly believe that God will try to salvage some good from our poor choices. One good thing is to learn from our mistakes.

> *And we know that God causes all things to work together for good to those who love God, to those who are called according to His purpose. (Romans 8:28)*

Perhaps God's Holy Spirit is planting the thought of Jeffery in that single mother's heart as comfort. Regardless, for the single mother or others who have regrets, no good comes from second-guessing the possibilities. Several times in C.S. Lewis' *The Chronicles of Narnia*[18], characters ask about alternative scenarios that could have resulted from other choices. The great lion Aslan lovingly explains, "No one is ever told what would have happened."

Although delivered by a God-like character, Aslan's words are not Scripture. Nevertheless, they ring true for nearly all situations. Perhaps the pain of knowing what could have happened would be too great for most of us to bear. This isn't to imply that we shouldn't learn from our experiences. On the contrary, we believe that God can use our memories to teach us, maybe even years after the event. Our mini-book *More Than Ordinary Wisdom: Stories of Faith and Folly* has engaging examples.

Some might read our admonition against second-guessing as an example of the "not doubting" requirement of James 1:5-6. No, James' words there apply to "not doubting" before God leads us to wisdom. Second-guessing occurs after choices have brought consequences and only occupies our hearts and thoughts.

> Have you been asking for wisdom? I have, for over a year. Have I been given wisdom? Yes, partially, as I have pursued wisdom by making phone calls, doing research, talking with Drew and others I trust. All of these should fill our time as we wait. Remember, wisdom is a pursuit. It is active.[19] (Kit Coons, *More Than Ordinary Abundance*)

We believe that this mini-book contains some biblical and practical ideas to improve one's ability to make good choices. The core principle is that applying the best understanding of Scripture we can achieve will lead to good decisions. We do not claim that this booklet is perfect. We offer it for your consideration. Remember the words of 1 Thessalonians 5:21 specifically related to wisdom from God says, "But examine everything carefully; hold fast to that which is good."

Our prayer for you is, "And this I pray, that your love may abound still more and more in real knowledge and all discernment." (Philippians 1:9) And there is no better choice for any person than the following:

You shall love the Lord your God with all your heart, and with all your soul, and with all your mind. This is the great and foremost commandment. The second is like it, You shall love your neighbor as yourself. On these two commandments depend the whole Law and the Prophets. (Matthew 22:37-40)

Bibliography

1. The Daily Walk (Illinois, Walk Thru the Bible Ministries, Volume 17, Number 3, March 1994).
2. Pascal Molenberghs, Fynn-Mathis Trautwein, Anne Böckler, Tania Singer, and Philipp Kanske. "Neural correlates of metacognitive ability and of feeling confident: a large-scale fMRI study" in Social, Cognitive and Affective Neuroscience. Published online July 21, 2016.
3. Moore, Beth. *James Mercy Triumphs*, Lifeway Press, 2011
4. Moore. *James Mercy Triumphs*.
5. Coons, Kit and Drew. *More Than Ordinary Wisdom: Stories of Faith and Folly*, 2018.
6. Mischel, Walter; Ebbesen, Ebbe B.; Raskoff Zeiss, Antonette (1972). *Cognitive and attentional mechanisms in delay of gratification*. Journal of Personality and Social Psychology.
7. Zigler, Zig. *Better Than Good: Creating a Life You Can't Wait to Live*. Thomas Nelson, 2007.
8. Coons, Kit and Drew. *More Than Ordinary Marriage: A Higher Level*, 2018.
9. Burkett, Larry. www.azquotes.com.
10. *USA Today*, February 28, 2018.
11. Moore. *James Mercy Triumphs*.
12. Moore. *James Mercy Triumphs*.
13. Coons, Kit and Drew. *More than Ordinary Faith: Why Does God Allow Suffering?* 2018.
14. E. Randolph Richards and Brandon J. O'Brien. *Misreading Scripture with Western Eyes—Removing Cultural Blinders to Better Understand the Bible*. InterVarsity Press, 2012.
15. Luther, Martin. *Von den Juden und ihren Lügen* (On the Jews and Their Lies), 1543.
16. St. Augustine. De doctrina christiana, Chapter 2.40.20.60.
17. Coons, Kit and Drew. *More Than Ordinary Challenges: Dealing with The Unexpected*.
18. Lewis, C.S. *The Chronicles of Narnia*.
19. Coons, Kit. *More Than Ordinary Abundance: From Kit's Heart*.

What is a more than ordinary life?

Each person's life is unique and special. In that sense, there is no such thing as an ordinary life. However, many people yearn for lives more special: excitement, adventure, romance, purpose, character. Our site is dedicated to the premise that any life can be more than ordinary.

At **MoreThanOrdinaryLives.com** you will find:

- inspiring stories
- ideas and resources
- entertaining novels
- free downloads

https://morethanordinarylives.com/

Challenge Series

by Kit and Drew Coons

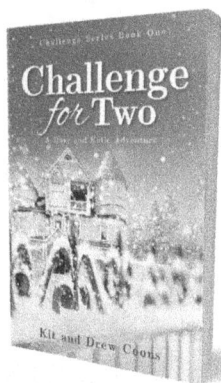

Challenge for Two

Book One

A series of difficult circumstances have forced Dave and Katie Parker into early retirement. Searching for new life and purpose, the Parkers take a wintertime job house sitting an old Victorian mansion. The picturesque river town in southeastern Minnesota is far from the climate and culture of their home near the Alabama Gulf Coast.

But dark secrets sleep in the mansion. A criminal network has ruthlessly intimidated the community since the timber baron era of the 19th century. Residents have been conditioned to look the other way.

The Parkers' questions about local history and clues they discover in the mansion bring an evil past to light and create division in the small community. While some fear the consequences of digging up the truth, others want freedom from crime and justice for victims. Faced with personal threats, the Parkers must decide how to respond for themselves and for the good of the community.

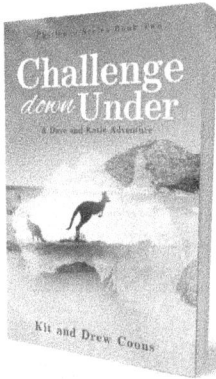

Challenge Down Under
Book Two

___

Dave and Katie Parker's only son, Jeremy, is getting married in Australia. In spite of initial reservations, the Parkers discover that Denyse is perfect for Jeremy and that she's the daughter they've always wanted. But she brings with her a colorful and largely dysfunctional Aussie family. Again Dave and Katie are fish out of water as they try to relate to a boisterous clan in a culture very different from their home in South Alabama.

After the wedding, Denyse feels heartbroken that her younger brother, Trevor, did not attend. Details emerge that lead Denyse to believe her brother may be in trouble. Impressed by his parents' sleuthing experience in Minnesota, Jeremy volunteers them to locate Trevor. Their search leads them on an adventure through Australia and New Zealand.

Unfortunately, others are also searching for Trevor, with far more sinister intentions. With a talent for irresponsible chicanery inherited from his family, Trevor has left a trail of trouble in his wake and has been forced into servitude. Can Dave and Katie locate him in time?

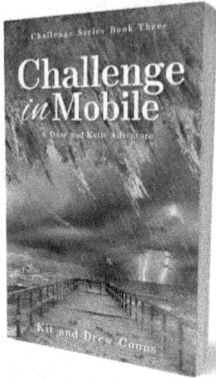

Challenge in Mobile
Book Three

Dave and Katie Parker regret that their only child Jeremy, his wife Denyse, and their infant daughter live on the opposite side of the world. Unexpectedly, Jeremy calls to ask his father's help finding an accounting job in the US. Katie urges Dave to do whatever is necessary to find a job for Jeremy near Mobile. Dave's former accounting firm has floundered since his departure. The Parkers risk their financial security by purchasing full ownership of the struggling firm to make a place for Jeremy.

Denyse finds South Alabama fascinating compared to her native Australia. She quickly resumes her passion for teaching inner-city teenagers. Invited by Katie, other colorful guests arrive from Australia and Minnesota to experience Gulf Coast culture. Aided by their guests, Dave and Katie examine their faith after Katie receives discouraging news from her doctors.

Political, financial, and racial tensions have been building in Mobile. Bewildering financial expenditures of a client create suspicions of criminal activity. Denyse hears disturbing rumors from her students. A hurricane from the Gulf of Mexico exacerbates the community's tensions. Dave and Katie are pulled into a crisis that requires them to rise to a new level of more than ordinary.

More from
Kit and Drew Coons

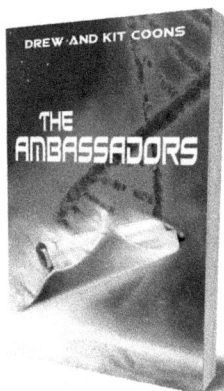

The Ambassadors

Two genetically engineered beings unexpectedly arrive on Earth. Unlike most extraterrestrials depicted in science fiction, the pair is attractive, personable, and telegenic—the perfect talk show guests. They have come to Earth as ambassadors bringing an offer of partnership in a confederation of civilizations. Technological advances are offered as part of the partnership. But humans must learn to cooperate among themselves to join.

Molly, a young reporter, and Paul, a NASA scientist, have each suffered personal tragedy and carry emotional baggage. They are asked to tutor the ambassadors in human ways and to guide them on a worldwide goodwill tour. Molly and Paul observe as the extraterrestrials commit faux pas while experiencing human culture. They struggle trying to define a romance and partnership while dealing with burdens of the past.

However, mankind finds implementing actual change difficult. Clashing value systems and conflicts among subgroups of humanity erupt. Inevitably, rather than face difficult choices, fearmongers in the media start to blame the messengers. Then an uncontrolled biological weapon previously created by a rogue country tips the world into chaos. Molly, Paul, and the others must face complex moral decisions about what being human means and the future of mankind.

more than
ORDINARY
lives
MINI SERIES

More Than Ordinary Challenges—
Dealing with the Unexpected

More Than Ordinary Marriage—
A Higher Level

More Than Ordinary Faith—
Why Does God Allow Suffering?

More Than Ordinary Wisdom—
Stories of Faith and Folly

More Than Ordinary Abundance—
From Kit's Heart

More Than Ordinary Choices—
Making Good Decisions

more than
ORDINARY
lives

Visit **https://morethanordinarylives.com/**
for more information.

About the Authors

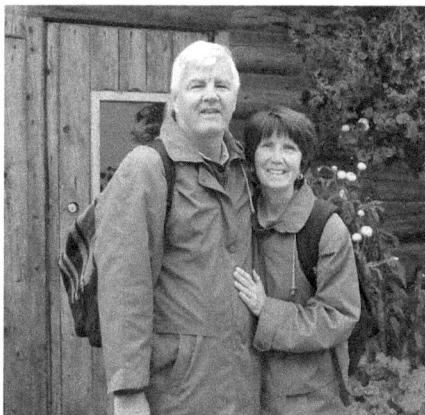

Kit and Drew Coons met while Christian missionaries in Africa in 1980. As humorous speakers specializing in strengthening relationships, they have taught in every part of the US and in thirty-nine other countries. For two years, the Coonses lived and served in New Zealand and Australia. They are keen cultural observers and incorporate their many adventures into their writing. Kit and Drew are unique in that they speak and write as a team.

www.ingramcontent.com/pod-product-compliance
Lightning Source LLC
Chambersburg PA
CBHW060536030426
42337CB00021B/4297